Much Wenlock Past to Present in Photographs

Much Wenlock Past to Present in Photographs

Book 2

Joy Sims and Ina Taylor

Ellingham Press
2012

The 'Doctor' was a familiar sight around Much Wenlock during 2012

British Library Cataloguing in Publication Data
A catalogue record for this book is available from the British Library

ISBN 978-0-9570781-5-4

Ellingham Press, 43 High Street, Much Wenlock, Shropshire TF13 6AD

Cover design and typesetting: Aardvark Illustration & Design (www.aardvarkid.co.uk)

Printed in Great Britain by Graphics and Print (Telford) Ltd

INTRODUCTION

Little did we think when we began working on *Much Wenlock Past to Present in Photographs* early in 2011 that there would be a need for a second book. We were more concerned about whether enough pictures existed for one book and whether people would be as interested as we were by them. The answer was an overwhelming yes! By the time we were ready to go to print we had amassed well over 500 pictures and now, a year later, we have reached 1500, with more still continuing to appear. This has meant that we have been lucky enough to have a great pool of material to draw on for exciting images of life in the town over the years.

In this volume we have continued some of the favourite themes with images of street scenes, schooldays and festive occasions but also allowed ourselves to travel a little further afield by including agriculture and quarrying, which were important occupations for many of Wenlock's inhabitants. We have also been able to look at the Barnardo's home and local schools which have closed down.

We haven't forgotten that this book is about the present as well as the past and so we have taken the opportunity to celebrate what an amazing year Much Wenlock has had in 2012. We hope you agree that our colourful cover says it all. Space prevents us from covering all the exciting and novel events that happened in the year; to do so would be a book in its own right.

Once again our biggest thanks go to the everyone in the community who has come forward with pictures and information about Wenlock life. Valerie Roberts, Jean Childs, Mike and Maureen Norrey, Betty Bebb and Glyn Williams deserve a special mention for putting in lots of time to help us understand what life in the town was like in the recent past and attempt to correct our misunderstandings. For that we are extremely grateful. And as before, we are very grateful to Suzanne Boulos for allowing us to draw on her extensive photographic archive of local activities. A list of formal acknowledgements and picture credits appears on page 96.

We have loved every minute of this journey through time and hope you find plenty to enjoy both past and present within these pages.

Ina Taylor & Joy Sims
October 2012

ABSTRACT OF RECEIPTS AND EXPENDITURE

OF THE

MUCH WENLOCK NATIONAL AND INFANT SCHOOLS.

FOR THE YEAR ENDING DECEMBER 31st, 1869.

Income.	£	s	d	*Expenditure.*	£	s	d
Balance	33	4	5	Salaries	201	15	9
Endowment	8	18	0	Books, &c.	27	3	0
Subscriptions	85	18	6	Fuel, Gas, &c.	6	7	9
School Pence	75	1	1	Repairs	5	7	4
Government Grant	74	4	0	Miscellaneous Expenses	4	8	10
Miscellaneous Receipts	10	8	0	Balance in hand...	42	11	4
	£287	14	0		£287	14	0

Examined—JOHN HORTON.

ANNUAL SUBSCRIPTIONS FOR 1869.

	£	s	d		£	s	d
The Right Hon. Lord Forester	10	0	0	Brought up	75	2	6
The Right Hon. Lord Wenlock	20	0	0	Rev. O. Fletcher	0	10	0
The Right Hon. General Forester, M. P.	5	0	0	Mrs. Furlong	1	0	0
A. H. Brown, Esq., M. P.	5	0	0	Mr. Hartland	0	3	0
James Milnes Gaskell, Esq.	20	0	0	Mr. Horton	0	10	0
Rev. W. H. Wayne	5	0	0	The Misses Horton	0	10	0
Mr. Adney	1	0	0	Mr. T. Instone	0	2	6
Mr. Amphlett	1	0	0	Madeley Wood Company	2	2	0
Mr. Blakeway	1	0	0	Rev. R. H. G. More	2	0	0
Mr. J. Bodenham	0	2	6	Mr. F. Moreton	0	10	0
Mr. Brookes	1	0	0	Mr. Owen	0	2	6
Miss Clively	0	5	0	Mrs. Owen	0	2	6
Mr. R. Cooper	1	0	0	Mr. H. P. Price	0	2	6
Messrs. Cooper and Purton	2	0	0	Mrs. Ray	1	1	0
Mr. C. J. Cooper	0	10	0	Mr. L. Reynolds	0	2	6
Mrs. Crowther	1	0	0	Mr. W. S. Reynolds	0	2	6
Mr. R. T. Davies	1	0	0	The Misses Seacome	1	0	0
Mr. T. P. Everall	0	2	6	Mr. H. Trevor	0	10	0
Mr. A. Fewtrell	0	2	6	Mr. H. Trevor, Jun.	0	5	0
	£75	2	6		£85	18	6

STATISTICS OF THE UPPER SCHOOL.

Number of Children on the books	156		Number who passed in Reading	131		
Average attendance for the year	128		„ „ „ „ Spelling and Writing	131		
Number qualified for examination	131		„ „ „ „ Arithmetic ...	131		
Number presented for examination	131		Number presented and passed in Geography, History, Grammar, and Composition ...	30		
Number of Infants on the books	144		Total number of Children on the books ...	300		

REPORT OF HER MAJESTY'S INSPECTOR.

March, 1870.

MIXED. "This School is not excelled by any School that I have ever inspected. The accuracy, neatness, and rapidity of the Elementary work, may without exaggeration be called surprising. These results are the more satisfactory, because no child has been kept back from Examination. The Scholars shew very great intelligence, and thoroughly understand what they read. Their History and Composition are very good, their Geography good, and their Grammar very fair. The Religious knowledge and Needlework deserve high praise. I was particularly pleased with the knowledge of the names and habits of birds displayed by the elder boys."

INFANTS. "The Infants are very well taught."

R. TEMPLE, H. M. Inspector.

JANE LAWLEY AND SON, PRINTERS AND STATIONERS, WENLOCK.

Inside the National School

The whole school has assembled for this photograph taken, it is thought, in June 1911 to commemorate the Coronation of George V. Through the glass partition, which separated the two classes in the larger room, union flags can be seen. Headteacher Mr Danks stands far right.

Medal for never having a day off school

Frederick William Lewis, aged 13, poses in his Sunday best, complete with pocket handkerchief, resplendent with the medal he was awarded for never missing a day's attendance at the National School. Absenteeism was a continual problem in Wenlock as in many rural areas because children were needed for seasonal agricultural work. Books and medals were given as an incentive to boost attendance.

High Street c. 1914

This view of the High Street from Ashfield Hall looks down towards the Swan & Falcon on the right (which became Barclays Bank in 1922). Also visible is William Anson the boot and shoe repairers. A gas light stands out from the wall at the side of the black and white cottage. Gas came to Much Wenlock courtesy of Dr William Penny Brookes amongst others.

Wilmore Street c. 1900

Not a great deal has changed in the hundred or more years since this photograph was taken apart from the removal of the spire on Holy Trinity and the railings around the churchyard. A solid wall now separates the Buttermarket from the passageway through to Church Walk.

Ashfield Hall

'Good Lodgings for Travellers' the board outside Ashfield Hall states, but local stories tell of it being a dosshouse in late Victorian times with some of the inmates sitting on the front wall picking off fleas. Appropriately the building is believed to be the site of the thirteenth-century St John's Hospital founded for 'lost and naked beggars'.

The Bark Peelers at Farley Sidings

Bark from oak trees was important for the tanning industry. Men felled trees in Bradley Coppice when the leaves began turning colour, then women and children peeled off the bark. The strips were collected by horse and cart and taken to Farley sidings. In this c. 1900 picture women fill the 'wiskets' (baskets) with bark ready for the men to clamber nimbly across planks to stack the strips of bark into 'ranks' to await collection by rail.

MUCH WENLOCK

SHROPSHIRE.

PARTICULARS OF VALUABLE FREEHOLD

RESIDENTIAL BUSINESS PROPERTY

Tannery, and Building Land,

VIZ: A

DESIRABLE AND COMMODIOUS RESIDENCE,

KNOWN AS

"THE TANYARD HOUSE,"

WITH

Drive, Shrubberies, Excellent Gardens, Stabling, Carriage House, Well-stocked Orchard, Capital Grass Land, Farm Buildings, &c.,

THE OLD-ESTABLISHED TANNERY,

COMPRISING—

Large Bark Barn, Scouring Rooms, Drying Rooms, Warehouses, Offices, Store Rooms, Mill Rooms, Beamhouse, Spacious Yards, Pits, Sheds, &c.,

TWO WELL-BUILT COTTAGES,

WITH GOOD GARDENS.

The House and Business Premises are very substantially built of Brick and Tile.   There is an abundant supply of excellent water.

The Property is very compact and well-situated, close to the Railway Station, with an extensive frontage for building sites both to Shineton Street and Station Road. It comprises in the whole 3A. 2R. 29P. or thereabouts.

MR. CHAS. E. AINSWORTH

HAS RECEIVED INSTRUCTIONS FROM MR. THOMAS ADNEY,

To offer the above for Sale by Auction,

AT

THE RAVEN HOTEL, MUCH WENLOCK,

ON

MONDAY, MARCH 23rd, 1891,

At THREE for FOUR o'clock, in the Afternoon, subject to Conditions to be then produced, and which will incorporate the Common Form Conditions of the Shropshire Law Society.

Particulars and Cards to View may be obtained from the AUCTIONEER, Much Wenlock; from Messrs. COOPER & HASLEWOOD, Solicitors, Much Wenlock and Bridgnorth; or from Mr. T. H. THORSFIELD, Land Agent, Barrow, Broseley.

NOTE.—Arrangements may be made, if convenient to the purchaser, that a portion (not exceeding two-thirds) of the purchase money may remain on mortgage of the Property.

Announcement of the tannery sale at the Raven in 1891 when 48-year-old owner Thomas Adney decided to retire to 1 Bourton Road (see page 18). Notice the details given of the Tanyard House pictured opposite.

The Bark Peelers at Farley Dingle

Wagons loaded with the bark strips are tipped out at Farley sidings ready for stacking. The left wheel runs up a plank whilst a pile of bark against the other protects the wheel as it goes over.

The Tanyard House, later known as the Red House

This building has had many uses. Once it was the home of tannery owner Thomas Adney who sold it to Miss Sophia Wayne, daughter of the vicar of Much Wenlock; she renamed it the Red House. In the Second World War it was used as a convalescent home for soldiers and later as the school canteen for pupils at school in the Bull Ring.

'A novel way of helping our wounded tommies', it said on this picture

Albert Brazier and Richard Davies pack up plants grown at the Abbey to sell as part of the Milnes Gaskells' effort to raise money for those wounded in the First World War.

Topiary at the Abbey

Topiary was particularly fashionable around the turn of the century and, as can be seen on these pages, the Milnes Gaskells set their gardeners to work creating various examples. Quite a few have survived to the present day.

Lawn-mowing at the Abbey

Kitty the donkey wears specially made leather shoes so she does not damage the lawns as she pulls the roller. Albert Brazier, Bill Bache and Richard Davies were gardeners at Wenlock Abbey. They also used Kitty to mow the bowling green on the Linden Field.

Wenlock Abbey

The Abbey, as it was officially known, was bought by James Milnes Gaskell in 1857. It became one of two homes of the Liberal MP and lawyer Charles Milnes Gaskell (the other being in Yorkshire) and after his death in 1919 passed to his wife Lady Catherine (daughter of the Earl of Portsmouth) who was a significant presence in the town.

Arriving in style

This early photograph of the Gaskell was taken before the matching bay window on the right was added. Mrs Jervis was the landlady at the time but the identity of the gentry arriving by carriage is not known.

Arriving at 1 Bourton Road

Tom Adney can be seen standing outside the door of his home Rindleford House. He moved there with his niece Fortune Sayce, seen standing alongside him in the garden, after the Tanyard House was sold (see page 14). The tall building in the background is the malt-house. Tom Craig is in the trap with his father.

The nursing staff at the Lady Forester Cottage Hospital

In this pre-First World War photograph the nursing staff (plus Matron's dog) sit outside the front door of the Lady Forester Cottage Hospital which had opened in 1902. Matron Smith sits in the front row with newly arrived Dr FW Hudson Bigley to the left. Dr Lockyer stands in the back row.

Sitting on the step in the Bull Ring

Two children sit outside 'John's Cottage', named after a former owner who was the 'whipper-in' at the church; his official job was to remove any dogs that ventured into the church. Between 1982 and 1984 the cottage was restored by the Historic Monument Trust and won a Civic Trust award in 1985.

The Lawn Tennis Club 1906

Members of the Lawn Tennis Club, to use their official title, pose in front of the nets on their two grass courts on the Linden Field. These courts over-lapped the running track and were situated behind the bowling green. The club gained a hard court in 1935 after Lady Catherine Milnes Gaskell gave the Linden Field to the town. Ladies not only played in long skirts at this time but were frequently expected to keep their hats on. Notice the shape of the tennis rackets.

Much Wenlock mixed hockey team 1926–7

Hockey thrived in the 1920s and 1930s with the town having a men's, a women's and a mixed team. Two men played at county level and one woman was reserve for the county. There was support from a high level in the town with Lady Catherine Milnes Gaskell one of the vice-presidents. Although the hockey pitch was on the Linden Field this photograph was taken behind the Talbot.

The Talbot Bowling Club in the 1920s

Bowling was another popular sport with two clubs in the town. The Linden Field Bowling Club (later Much Wenlock Bowling Club) began in the 1860s followed by the Talbot Bowling Club whose green was behind the Talbot pub in the High Street. Today this club is remembered in the road name Bowling Green Way.

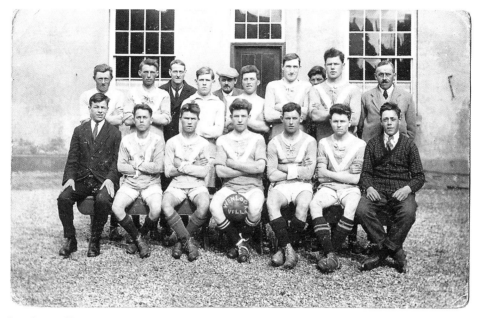

Wenlock Villa Football Team

'Football has had its ups and downs in Wenlock,' the local paper reported in 1936. Much of this was put down to the fact they didn't have their own pitch. Wenlock Villa (photographed at the back of the Stork pub in Wilmore Street c. 1930) played on the cricket pitch but this was stopped in 1933 because of damage to the pitch. Football was then moved to the racecourse but this was never popular because the pitch sloped downhill. After 1935 the football team received its own pitch on the newly donated Gaskell Field.

Much Wenlock Cycling Club 1922
This early group of cyclists are pictured outside the newly converted Memorial Hall. The building had previously been an open market hall.

Stentiford's the plumbers

Many a Much Wenlock toilet cistern bore the name of Stentiford, who were plumbers and 'fitters of gas and hot water' to the town's inhabitants between 1922 and the 1940s. The sign on their window at 53 High Street is in rather a sad state.

The vanished shop

Smith & Co was a general stores at the top of the High Street. It was demolished in the late 1930s, along with the Harp pub on the corner, when the Bridgnorth Road was widened. Smith & Co also had premises in Ludlow and Craven Arms.

Hunters Tea Stores

Hunters Tea Stores opened at 7 High Street in 1909; it was one of their chain of stores trading across the midlands and north. They sold their own-brand tea as well as groceries and items of hardware like tin baths, pots and pans. The state of the assistant's overall in this 1920s photograph doesn't inspire too much confidence!

45 Sheinton Street

Gertrude Davies (born 1869) stands in the cottage doorway. Her husband Richard was a gardener at Wenlock Abbey (see page 16). The railway bridge is visible in the left of the picture. Some years later a lorry going down New Road lost control and practically demolished the cottage by the bridge. Fortunately no one was hurt.

Railway Cottage, Sheinton Street

Changes to the front of this cottage make it harder to recognise today but it is still there even though the railway it took its name from has gone. During the 1960s and 1970s the little door to the left of the picture led into a hairdresser's.

Road to Ruins

Early motorists were warned this was the 'Road to Ruins' and that there was 'No room for wagons or charabancs to turn' if they ventured any further towards the Priory ruins. The main entrance to the Milnes Gaskell residence at Wenlock Abbey is just visible to the right of the man. The noticeboard advises people they can visit the ruins on a Sunday afternoon at a cost of 6d (2½p).

Heavy horses work at Spoonhill

Eight horses haul timber at Spoonhill shortly before the First World War, under the direction of chief horseman Bert Lister. Once the First World War started most horses were removed for war service, leaving farmers with only one to do all their work.

Harvesting at Wyke Farm c. 1938

Percy Whiteman is cutting the wheat at Wyke Farm shortly before the outbreak of World War II. His Fordson Standard tractor has been attached to the old horse binder.

Feeding the animals

Bryan Bebb, along with twins Betty and Ron, takes the feed to the animals on their farm at Atterley.

Haymaking at Newtown Farm 1938

Haymaking in Stackyard Meadow on Charles Hill's farm.

Harvest Home c. 1911

The harvest is in and the Patton House Farm wagon is packed with the family and employees of Jesse Wadlow, dressed in their Sunday best, ready to make their way to the Harvest Festival service at Stanton Long church. The wagon is decorated with corn-dollies.

Hay harvest in

Aaron Lloyd and his son Jack pose with the horse that has brought their hay crop in.

Harvest c. 1950

Mrs Bebb packed all the food in the wash basket to go up the field for lunch during harvest. Crockery was at the bottom, cake next, then a linen cloth and the sandwiches. Every year the Morris family, seen here in the middle, came from Birmingham to join in the harvest at Atterley.

Harvest auction

Produce was collected at the Talbot, then auctioned. The money raised was used to buy items like sugar and tea to give to 'the elderly and deserving poor' in Much Wenlock.

The Racecourse

This 1922 photograph is a rare picture of a meeting at Wenlock Races. The course opened on this site, close to the present-day primary school, early in the nineteenth century and closed in 1939.

The Wenlock Farmers' Club (founded 1842) had an annual show on the racecourse where the best hunters and shires were judged. This was one of the oldest shows in the country and many local farmers competed. John Grainger took great pride in showing his horses.

The Smithy

Tom Evans ran this blacksmith's in Victoria Road, the other smithy run by Choppy Hanson was in St Mary's Lane. Both blacksmiths adapted their trade to repairing agricultural machinery as the use of horses declined.

Jack Lloyd outside 43 High Street

The horse and cart was a familiar sight in the High Street in earlier times. The Lloyd family were immensely proud of the heavy horses and groomed them to perfection for any parade in the town.

Much Wenlock
Railway Station 1933

The railway, opened in 1862, was the life-blood of the town, transporting people, goods and animals far and wide. Its closure under the Beeching cuts in the mid 1960s changed the town's development for ever.

Homer School

Homer School was designed by Pountney-Smith, architect of Wenlock's market hall and police station, in 1859. Once pupils reached the age of eight they had to move to the National School in the Bull Ring. In 1917 Homer school closed. The whole school is pictured here in 1904, the year sixty-year-old Miss Elizabeth Harling retired.

Bourton School

The redbrick school at Bourton opened in 1878 and closed in July 1967.

Brockton School

Brockton National School opened in 1844 and closed on that site in 1971, when teachers and pupils moved to their present building. Pupils in this c. 1939 photograph stand outside the original building which has now been converted into a house.

The School in the Bull Ring

Some of the pupils who attended Wenlock Elementary School, in the Bull Ring, in 1926. Mr Alec Findlayson was the master in charge, assisted by Miss Lovatt, the infant mistress.

The scouts' and guides' Christmas party 1931

The scouts met in the ATC hut in New Road but later moved to the Raven hut, a wooden structure in St Mary's Road behind the hotel.

The 1st Wenlock Scout Troop c. 1940

Scoutmaster Fred Kleenlyside, who was also a teacher, poses with the scouts at the back of Corris House. The Barnardo's Home ran a very successful scout troop which boys from the town also joined. They had their own scout hut in which they kept musical instruments and flags. There was space enough for the boys to practise boxing, club-swinging and darts.

Much Wenlock Cub Pack c. 1971

The cub pack was started at Corris House by Mrs Kitchen; by the time of this photograph Margaret Attwood was Akela and ran the pack helped by Kate Cooper and Liz Adkins.

Preparing for Civic Sunday

Mrs Firmstone's cat came to investigate why the cubs, scouts, guides and brownies were assembling outside the church in May 1985. Bill Pratt was the standard-bearer for the Royal British Legion.

The Home Guard

Much Wenlock Home Guard was based in the garage in the Talbot yard. This photograph shows a small number of them outside the Horse & Jockey pub (known locally as the Bonnets). Their very basic uniform without webbing belts or gaiters, as well as the First World War bandolier (for carrying ammunition), suggest this picture dates from early in the war and is made up of locals from the Bonnets area who were assembling ready to march into town to join the others at the Talbot. Their leader here is 'Stick' Langford, a quarry worker who had served in the Boer War and the First World War.

The women members of Much Wenlock Fire Service

By 1944 there were 14 firewomen in all. Although they are standing outside the garage of the Raven, they were based at a hut on the corner near the Gaskell Hotel.

A wartime wedding

Lily Clissold marries at Holy Trinity Church. The family lived at 2 the Bull Ring and her
father was a signalman at Much Wenlock station.

Unveiling the war memorial

On 11 November 1948 a memorial to the allied airmen killed in the Borough of Wenlock
during the Second World War was unveiled in the Guildhall. At the top of the memorial
there is a clock and below are listed the names of those killed, the majority being Ameri-
cans. Town Clerk George Matthews stands behind the Mayor Cllr Parslow and Cllr Lewis
Motley is on the right of the picture.

The quarrymen

After blasting had taken place in the quarry, the limestone blocks were broken by hand with sledgehammers. Very large pieces had small charges put under them to split them again. This group of men smashed limestone up to be loaded into tubs and taken away by horse and cart.

A lime worker

In this pre-Second World War photograph, the man stands in front of an adit. His job was to shovel lime powder (calcium oxide) from the bottom of the kiln into the cart (visible right behind him). The horse and cart would take it off for agricultural use.

Farley quarry

Hunks of limestone were tipped into the primary crusher (to the right in this picture) to be broken into smaller lumps. These moved up the conveyor belt to be milled into powder which then travelled along into the hoppers to be tipped into waiting lorries.

New lorry for Coates Quarry August 1960

Bill Whitfield drives Jemson's newly delivered yellow lorry to collect powdered lime from the Coates quarry for agricultural use. Sixpence a ton was paid to the landowner for every ton of lime taken from this quarry. Bill, who lived at Perkley's Farm, was the local AA patrolman at one time.

The old railway bridge

Ian Firmstone stands by Roger Willis on the tricycle on the Stretton Road. This is one of the few pictures to show the old railway bridge before its demolition.

Playing in the Mutton Shut c. 1950

Stan Clerk, Alan Palgrave, Margaret Palgrave, Richard Matthews and Alan Matthews at play with their homemade truck.

A real-life *Gone to Earth* star?

Shades of *Gone to Earth* in this 1952 photograph of Honor Brazier cuddling Chapper the fox. Her father had found him as a cub and Honor reared him as a pet. Chapper was permitted to sleep in the coal hole at the farmhouse.

"The Archers Film Productions"

"GONE TO EARTH"

PRODUCED AND DIRECTED BY
MICHAEL POWELL AND EMERIC PRESSBURGER

Sequences from the above film, to be made in Technicolor and based on Mary Webb's well-known Novel,

WILL BE FILMED IN THIS DISTRICT DURING THE WEEK

COMMENCING

11TH JULY, 1949.

There will be VACANCIES for approximately 70 persons as extras, composed of elderly, middle aged and young people, and boys and girls. Anyone wishing to APPLY FOR AN AUDITION should submit details in writing of age, name & address to the Town Clerk.

WOMEN SHOULD PREFERABLY HAVE LONG HAIR

PERSONS WHO ARE IN POSSESSION OF CLOTHES OF THE PERIOD ABOUT 1900 SHOULD MAKE A NOTE OF THIS WHEN GIVING THEIR PARTICULARS

ANY FURTHER INFORMATION MAY BE OBTAINED FROM ME

A. G. MATTHEWS

TOWN CLERK'S OFFICE
MUCH WENLOCK
SHROPSHIRE

TOWN CLERK

SLATER & CO. PRINTERS IRONBRIDGE

The traction engine

Known locally as the 'steamer', this traction engine was being taken out for filming a scene for *Gone to Earth* and driven by local Bernard Alderson. Film star Jennifer Jones can be seen in the cart passing a road sign.

Gone to Earth stars in the Mutton Shut

Jennifer Jones, along with Mike Powell the director, relaxing between filming in the Mutton Shut in 1949.

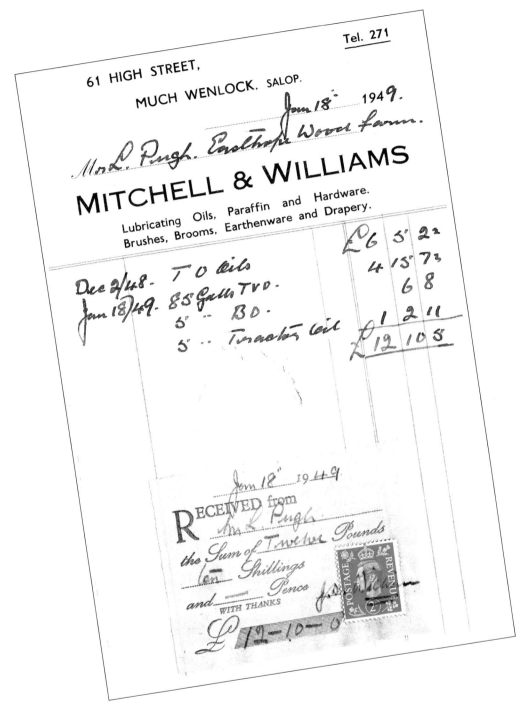

Receipt from Mitchell & Williams, 61 High Street

Behind his premises (today the Copper Kettle tearooms), Mr Williams stored 5,000 gallons of highly flammable fuel oils. The receipt shows 85 gallons of TVO (tractor vaporising oil) used in tractors, 5 gallons of BO (burning oil was a cheaper grade of Esso blue) and 5 gallons of tractor oil for lubricating the sumps on tractors.

One of Mr Williams' lorries in Back Lane
This lorry was a Canadian Dodge because it was impossible to buy a new British lorry after the Second World War.

At the Gaskell junction
The policeman stands in the middle of the junction in this early 1930s photograph before the Bridgnorth Road was widened.

1948 Carnival

Carnival Queen Betty Hatchman sits with her attendants on the dray that has arrived on the Linden Field after processing through the town. Dark-haired Joyce Duckett sitting far right was a stand-in for Jennifer Jones (see page 45) during *Gone to Earth* filming. The football pavilion on the Gaskell Field can be seen in the background and the beer tent to the left.

A farmer's float

The placard 'We help feed the nation' strikes a serious note in this pre-Second World War photograph of the carnival parade. Horses were always beautifully turned out and farm wagons used as drays. Lorries replaced the wagons later. Behind the farmer to the right, the water tower on the goods yard is visible.

Assembled for judging

A float on the station goods yard prepares to join the carnival procession through the town. A train can be seen behind them.

Pick of the Pops 1955

The float waits for the judges on the coal yard at the beginning of the carnival. The houses of Southfield Road, as well as coal heaps and a goods van, can be seen in the background.

1948 Carnival float

This beautiful float, which took Sleeping Beauty as its theme, is also assembling on the coal yard and the cottages of Mardol Terrace can be seen behind.

Corris House, 13 Southfield Road

The plaque above the door reads, 'Dr Barnardo's Home, Wenlock Branch. The gift of Alderman T Cook JP and Mr T Morris, 1929'. It was not until 1937 that the building became known as Corris House in honour of its founders; prior to that it had been called Windy Ridge.

Marching out

The 'home boys', as locals called them, were a familiar sight marching in pairs down to the town. On a Sunday, some wore their scout or cub uniforms when they marched down to church.

Group assembled in 1952

When the Home opened it was designed to cater for 52 boys aged between 6 and 15 years.

Going to camp

During World War II, the boys were taken camping on Wenlock Edge. In this later photograph they are taking their mattresses out to pack on the lorry ready for summer camp by the sea.

Roadworks

The installation of the sewerage system in the Stretton Road in 1912 was a noteworthy
event in the lives of the local inhabitants. Several families have assembled outside Yew Tree
Cottage to be photographed alongside the pipes in this £5000 improvement scheme.

Repairs to the Bull Ring *(top right)*

Major street diversions were caused by work in Wilmore Street and Sheinton Street in 1981
aimed at alleviating the effects of flooding. Sadly the 2007 floods still overwhelmed the
drainage here.

Improvements to the culvert in the High Street

Substantial work was undertaken in 2003 to improve the culvert under the High Street.

Much Wenlock

To get your bearings in this
aerial photograph c. 1948, it may
help to identify Wenlock Abbey in the
top right quarter of the picture and the
railway line in the top left quarter. Two
gasometers can be seen in the bottom right-hand
corner with the Milnes-Motley factory
behind them.

The Raven and the Plough

This photograph of Barrow Street, dating from the 1930s, shows not only the Raven Hotel but also the Plough pub, whose sign can be seen jutting out close to the car.

The Bonnets

The Horse & Jockey pub up the Stretton Road was known locally as the Bonnets. Edward Horn, the licensee in 1913, is seen outside.

Cider presses at George & Dragon in the 1950s

The George & Dragon brewed its own cider and perry in the past and the brewer can be seen on the right of the picture. He also worked behind the bar in the evening. The man on the left fills in paperwork after testing the strength of the liquor in the barrels.

Tipplers at the Talbot

This happy group are drinking in the Talbot yard. Landlady Lavinia 'Letty' Dalby is the woman wearing glasses on the back row.

Inside the Parish Room c. 1952

Headteacher Phillip Barber goes over Richard Matthews' work in the Parish Room which was part of the headmaster's house (now the Old Savings Bank) at the top of the Bull Ring. The 'teacher's pet' from this period remembers her special morning task was to go and buy Mr Barber ten Woodbines and a box of matches from the High Street, whilst the rest of the class got on with Bible-reading.

School 1953–4

Mr Barber, with his class the following year, has moved to the HORSA huts on the Gaskell Field.

Much Wenlock Modern School

Forty-four pupils pose with their teacher at the top of the games field behind the Much Wenlock Modern School soon after its opening in 1953.

The class of 1970

The closure of the school in the Bull Ring caused some pupils to be sent to the newly constructed HORSA huts on the edge of the games field. A few went to the Parish Room (opposite) until enough HORSA huts were built. The primary school transferred to Racecourse Lane in 1973. This photograph above captures the whole school in the HORSA huts on 16 February 1970.

ATHLETIC
TEAMS
1958

Physical education in the new Wenlock Modern School

Young sporting talent has always been supported in the town and borough since the days of Dr William Penny Brookes who pioneered physical education in schools.

Cricket in Wenlock

The town has a long history of cricket but sadly few photographs have survived of the teams. This is the Much Wenlock Cricket Club 2nd XI in the early 1990s.

Wenlock women's cricket team

The men need not be too scared. This group of ladies formed themselves into a cricket team on one occasion only on 27 September 1959 in order to challenge the men. The score is not recorded.

Opening the Legion Hall 22 October 1949

The Wenlock British Legion branch opened their own hall in Smithfield Road in 1949.
Lt-Gen Oliver Lees (at the microphone) performed the ceremony. Mrs Ward, whose family
owned the land, is on the left, and Capt Kane (chairman of the Hall and a quarry
owner whose limestone was used in the building) sits on the other side with Dr FW Hudson
Bigley. Mrs Landon, President of the Women's Legion, is far right.

The Horticultural Show

Kenny Milner and Mike 'Peony' Pearce admiring the prize vegetables which have won the cup. The horticultural show was a regular part of the Olympian Games weekend during the 50s, and many said that those living at Havelock Crescent were the best gardeners.

Flower show 1961 *(left)*

The Wenlock Horticultural Society was formed in 1898 under the patronage of the Milnes Gaskells at Wenlock Abbey. The annual show was held in mid August on the Linden Field with entertainment from the Boy Scouts and drill and horse-vaulting displays by soldiers from Shrewsbury barracks. The flower show continued and here on 23 September 1961 Mrs Ward (daughter of Lady Catherine Milnes Gaskell) awards a prize to Mr Dennis Childs.

Wenlock Male Voice Choir

Joe Platt suggested forming a male voice choir in 1968 and the initial meeting took place in the Stork Room in Wilmore Street, where the group first began practising the following year. They transferred to the upstairs of the Corn Exchange and then, assisted by Norman Wood, the choir became 'a night-school class' enabling them to rehearse at the secondary school where they still are today. Ceridwen Constantine, the musical director, sits on the right with accompanist Beryl Malone.

The sexton

A one-and-a-quarter-acre cemetery, with its own chapel, was established on the Bridgnorth Road in 1890 (at a cost of £1200) when the churchyard became full.

The Sunday School

Sunday School in the Methodist Church in King Street around 1965. In 1960 the Sheinton Street Chapel (now Wenlock Pottery) closed and a joint Sunday School was formed in the newly renovated Sunday School Room in King Street.

St Mary Magdalene RC Church

At first a Catholic chapel was set up in a room above the Post Office at 7 Sheinton Street. Then, as numbers grew, in 1935 James Bowden converted his disused malt-house behind the Post Office into the Chapel of St Milburga. Later the newly built St Mary Magdalene Church opened on 4 October 1955 at the end of Barrow Street.

The Madonna and Child statue

This statue was brought to Wenlock on the coach by evacuees from Liverpool during World War II. It was all that survived from a bombed-out church.

Dave Merrick and Roman Hoard

On 13 October 1977, when David Merrick was ploughing at Westwood Farm for David Craig, he spotted a mass of old coins in the furrow. The find was reported and subsequent archaeology unearthed over 3000 Roman coins, the equivalent of one Roman's life savings. The British Museum investigated the hoard and at the inquest in Telford it was decided the coins belonged to the finder and landowner.

Extra-curricular activities

Between 1955 and 1962 WA Silvester, a teacher at Much Wenlock Modern School, excavated a fourth-century Roman villa at Yarchester, near Harley, with staff and pupils. They uncovered a high-status villa with six rooms and a well-preserved mosaic floor.

Skeletons in the Bull Ring

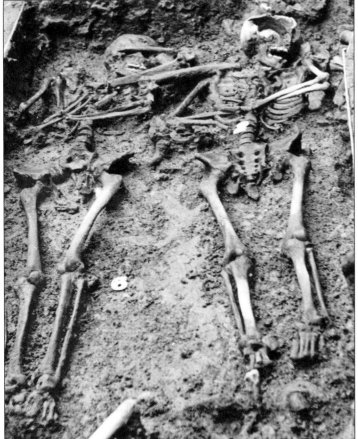

During the 1980s renovations to the mid-sixteenth-century cottages in the Bull Ring revealed nine burials which came right up to the cottage back walls. Given the proximity to the churchyard this was not surprising. All were correctly excavated, recorded and re-interred.

A view up the Shrewsbury Road

Postman Percy Chamberlain, who lived in the first cottage on the left of the road, bought damsons from the locals. He sold them on for use in the fabric-dyeing industry in Manchester, courtesy of trains from Wenlock station.

Where do you fork right for Shrewsbury?

The road sign on this photograph makes it hard to get your bearings because today's road priorities have changed. Once you realise George Cooke is standing outside the Pound, things become clearer.

Bridge at Southfield Road

Archaeologist Mark Horton, then a Wilmore Street resident, successfully fought to preserve this railway bridge. He argued that Wenlock's railway heritage was every bit as important as its medieval heritage and that relatively few such bridges remained. The bridge, built between 1861 and 1864, comprises cast-iron beams, jack arches and stone abutments. Some argued for its demolition to make a safer access but Dr Horton said the hump-back bridge acted as a traffic calmer.

Civic Sunday 23 November 1947

Civic Sunday was always an important date in the Borough of Wenlock's calendar, when the newly installed mayor attended the church service. Here the mayor is Councillor Walter Parslow (who lived in Mardol House) with his wife; town clerk George Matthews stands next to the mace-bearer. The British Legion flags are carried by Mr Kitson and Mrs Hollinshead.

The British Legion parade July 1985

There was a strong British Legion presence in Much Wenlock from 1931 and parades from the Legion Hall to the church were an annual event supported, as here, by different branches of the Legion around the county.

Civic parade May 1965

Mayors and civic dignitaries from all Shropshire boroughs came to Much Wenlock for the presentation of the Honorary Freedom of the Borough of Wenlock to the King's Shropshire Light Infantry. They are seen here processing to the Gaskell Field for the ceremony. Notice the former Stork Hotel at the top of the Bull Ring.

Freedom of the Borough of Wenlock 1965

The King's Shropshire Light Infantry parade up the High Street on 23 May 1965 after the ceremony in which Mayor Cllr Derek Hill presented the Colonel of the Regiment with a scroll and casket. To exercise the Freedom of Entry the regiment paraded through the streets past the Guildhall and up the High Street.

Much Wenlock Fire Crew 1944

Wenlock's Fire Chief sitting in the centre was town clerk George Matthews, and on the left sits the Chief Fire Officer from Shrewsbury. The Fire Station was situated up the Bridgnorth Road at this time.

A call-out c. 1960

Fireman Kenneth Milner hoses down a pile of burning tyres at a garage fire on the river front in Shrewsbury.

Award Winners 1964
Much Wenlock Fire Brigade pose after winning a competition. L to R: Cyril Evans, Sid Minton, Jack Clayton, Gordon James and John Baugh (whose son is below).

The Crew of 2012
From left to right: Danny Mills, Brad Kingsley, Chris Davies, Alistair Humphries (watch manager), Danny Hurst (crew manager), Michael Baugh. Front: Sean Nicholas (crew manager).

A Day in Much Wenlock

On 14 May 1981 RAF Cosford sent a group of students on a photographic course to Much Wenlock for the day. Their archive, which was given to the town afterwards, is a wonderful snapshot of life on one particular day. Here, and opposite, are some of those pictures.

Serving petrol in Smithfield Road

When the Bridgnorth Road was widened, Bache's petrol station moved from its position against the Gaskell wall to this site in Smithfield Road. Mrs George Bache is seen here filling up a car. The pay kiosk can just be glimpsed behind the pumps.

Morris Corfield's yard

After the railway closed, agricultural engineers Morris Corfield moved onto this site in the 1960s. With the increasing size of agricultural machinery the firm moved their main depot to Broseley in 2010.

Top of the Bull Ring

The shop on the corner of the Bull Ring had to operate under Mrs Martin's name because her husband was manager of Phillips the grocer's in the High Street. The Stork public house can be seen to the right.

Windmill before renovation

The sad state of the windmill before restoration began in 2006. Along with conserving the structure, a proper door was fitted and the crenellations (a fanciful Victorian addition in a parlous state) were removed.

Work in progress

Much Wenlock Windmill Trust was formed in 2001 to secure and preserve the remaining shell of the windmill. Mike Norrey spent a great deal of time and energy working on the shell and later researching its history.

All calm and complete
Ponies graze contentedly on Windmill Hill alongside the preserved windmill.

Restoration of the clock in the Square
The Town Council commissioned the restoration of the cast-iron casing of the Cooke clock. Work was carried out at the Jackfield Conservation Studios in 1993 by Lesley Durbin, who became Mayor of Much Wenlock in 2011.

Well-dressing in Wenlock (1996–2006)

Jane Williams took over the well-dressing of St Owen's and St Milburgha's wells from Dorothy Smith. Inspired by visits to Derbyshire, Jane collected a band of volunteers, male and female. Men built the wooden frames, then took them down to Farley Brook to soak for a couple of weeks (weighted down by rocks to stop them floating away). The saturated frames returned to Wenlock where they were put in Alan Henn's garage and people began filling them with clay collected from the Pottery. Jane's full-sized designs on brown paper (pinned on the wall) were pricked out on the clay with a knitting needle and black wool pushed into the clay to define the design. For the rest of the week women worked at adding the petals, beans, bark and organic materials to create the picture.

The finished designs were incredibly heavy and some of the firemen helped carry the design into place.

A ceremony to bless the gift of water took place on the Friday evening.

High Causeway before demolition 1968–9

Originally plans were drawn up to preserve these cottages by converting them into three family dwellings (rent £2 a week) or old people's flats (£1 a week). Sadly the plans came to nothing and in 1968 they were bulldozed.

Catholic church comes down

Falling attendance, shortage of priests and rising costs led to the Catholic church closing on 3 February 2008. It was demolished in 2012, along with the adjacent priest's house, and new houses have been built on the site.

The end of the Legion Hall

Demand for a British Legion Hall continued to fall in the twenty-first century leading to its closure and the site being put up for sale.

At the beginning of 2012 the bulldozers moved in and cleared the area. By the middle of the year two houses had sprung up.

30 May 2012: the day the Olympic Torch came to Wenlock

The Council get the bunting out.

A Merry Wife of Windsor

The choice of play for the Wenlock Festival in the Queen's Jubilee year was obvious: it had to be *The Merry Wives of Windsor*. Here Mistress Page (acted by Angela Beechey) performed on the church green in June 2012.

Monte Carlo comes to Wenlock

As part of the Wenlock Festival a parade of the most creative wheelbarrow, followed by a race around the streets, was first introduced in 2010. Christine Greeve, seen on that occasion, gets ready to run with her decorated wheelbarrow.

Welcome Songs 11 July 2012

Much Wenlock was chosen as one of four locations to host the Welcome Songs as part of the Cultural Olympiad. Crowds arrived at Wenlock Priory to hear Eliza Carthy and I Fagiolini along with local artists and choirs.

The Herald returns

For the first time in fifty years, the Wenlock Olympian Games had a herald mounted on a white pony to lead athletes along the High Street to the Gaskell Field.

The Herald's Procession

Wenlock Olympian athlete, Kevin Evans, waves as the procession approaches the Gaskell Field. Kevin continued his success by winning the cup for the seven-mile race for the sixth year in succession.

Olympic Gliding

This was a first for Wenlock Olympian Games but one they hope will be repeated and lead the way to the sport becoming part of the international Olympics. Although most of the action took place on the Long Mynd, gliders flew over the Gaskell Field and some landed there.

First Olympian Marathon

Jonathan Edwards presented the medals to winners of the first Wenlock Olympian Marathon and Half Marathon.

Torchbearer

John Simpson, an Olympic torchbearer on 30 May, holds his torch in front of the memorial to Dr William Penny Brookes. Underneath the Victorian memorial, another was placed in 2012 to commemorate the doctor's role in the modern Olympic revival.

2012 Wow what a year!

Tim King, Shropshire Tourism Officer, was regularly in town with foreign journalists.

The museum opened in February after a big renovation.

In July the Poetry Parnassus was held in the Pottery as part of the 2012 Cultural Olympiad.

MP Philip Dunne unveiled the Olympic-inspired Public Art Trail in July.

The poetry stone was placed on the church green.

Anna (daughter of Megan Morris-Jones) and her husband Sean will take over Cuan House Wildlife Rescue.

ACKNOWLEDGEMENTS

Joy and Ina are very grateful to the Town Council for allowing them access to the town archives for research purposes, under the very able guidance of Howard Horsley, Honorary Archivist. We also acknowledge the help given us by Shropshire Museum Service, through Emma-Kate Lanyon, and their kindness in allowing us to reproduce photographs in their collection. We wish to thank Julia Bailey and the Friends of Much Wenlock Museum for assisting us with information and pictures. We are also grateful to Tom Foxall for allowing us to reproduce the pictures on pages 90 and 91; Shropshire County Council for the picture on page 94; the Press Association and LOCOG for permission to reproduce the front cover photograph of the Olympic Torch in the High Street; Wenlock Olympian Society for permission to use the pictures on pages 4, 88, 89, 92 and 93; Paul and Sabine Hutchison of Virtual Shropshire for allowing us to reproduce their Olympian pictures; Lesley Durbin for the photograph on page 83.

The majority of the photographs, along with their fascinating stories, have come to us from local residents. To all these people – too many to name – we say a very big thank you: we could not have produced this book without you.

Some other local books you might be interested in.

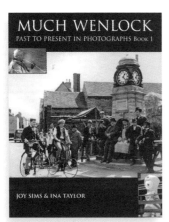

Much Wenlock
Past to Present Book 1

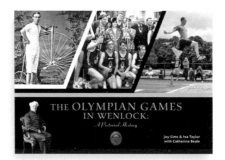

The Olympian Games in Wenlock

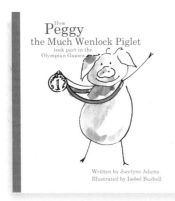

Peggy the Much Wenlock Piglet

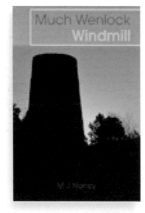

Much Wenlock Windmill